D1394876

OXFORD
UNIVERSITY PRESS

Great Clarendon Street, Oxford OX2 6DP

Oxford University Press is a department of the University of Oxford.
It furthers the University's objective of excellence in research, scholarship,
and education by publishing worldwide. Oxford is a registered trade mark of
Oxford University Press in the UK and in certain other countries

Designed by Jo Cameron
Edited by Clare Whitston and Liz Cross

British Library Cataloguing in Publication Data

Data available

ISBN: 978-0-19-273458-7

1 3 5 7 9 10 8 6 4 2

Printed in Great Britain by Bell and Bain Ltd, Glasgow

Paper used in the production of this book is a natural,
recyclable product made from wood grown in sustainable forests.
The manufacturing process conforms to the environmental
regulations of the country of origin.

JINKS & O'HARE
FUNFAIR REPAIR

BY PHILIP REEVE
AND
SARAH MCINTYRE

OXFORD
UNIVERSITY PRESS

ONE

Emily could sleep through almost any noise, but silence always woke her. That was because she lived on Funfair Moon, and it was usually pretty noisy.

Funfair Moon has the highest helter-skelters, the longest roller coasters, the bounciest trampolines, the scariest ghost train and the most delicious candyfloss in the entire galaxy. Every night, as Emily drifted off to sleep in her little bedroom above the Lost Property Office, she could hear the sounds of the fair going on outside. 'Wheeee!'

went thousands of people hurtling down the helter-skelters. 'Waaaaaargh!' went thousands more, riding the roller coasters. 'WooooooOOOOooo!' went the scary music from the ghost train. *Boingggggg* went the trampolines. And from far and wide the noises of the other rides came drifting—*Whoosshhh, PING, ker-CHUNG-ga ker-CHUNG-ga.* (The candyfloss didn't make much noise, but Emily could smell it. The sweet, burnt-sugar scent came creeping through her window and into her dreams.)

Emily loved that funfair din. It was like a lullaby to her, soothing her softly off to sleep every night. When she woke next morning, everything would be quiet, except maybe for a litter-picker whistling as he gathered up torn tickets and crumpled sweet wrappers from the grassy paths between the roundabouts. The rides were closed, and Funfair Moon was preparing for new visitors, and another day and night of noisy fun.

Most of the people who lived on Funfair Moon lived in little houses next to the rides they ran, but Emily had always lived in the Lost Property Office. One night, almost ten years before, some over-excited visitor had laid a large, pale-blue egg on the Switchback of Doom, one of Funfair Moon's biggest roller coasters. There it had been found next morning by the fair's hard-working repair men, Jinks and O'Hare. Mr Jinks had said that it was probably scrambled after riding around on the Switchback of Doom all night, but Mr O'Hare had made him bring it to the Lost Property Office anyway.

Mrs Mimms, who was in charge of all the lost property, stuck a label on it and put it on a shelf among all the hats and umbrellas and space suits which were waiting there for their owners to come back for them.

But nobody ever came to claim the pale-blue egg. Whoever it was who left it on the Switchback of Doom must have forgotten about it. When it hatched, and little Emily crawled out, Mrs Mimms had not been quite sure what to do with her, but Jinks and O'Hare had turned the attic into a bedroom, and Emily had lived there happily ever since.

She kept the fragments of the pale-blue eggshell on her bedside shelves, among her books and toys, but she hardly ever bothered wondering if anyone would come back for it. It seemed to Emily that the sort of people who went to all the trouble of laying large, pale-blue eggs and then just left them lying about on roller coasters probably wouldn't make very good parents anyway. She was pretty happy living on her own. Mrs Mimms, who ran the Lost Property Office, wasn't exactly like a mum. In fact, she was more like a sort of giant alien octopus. But she was a very nice giant alien octopus, and didn't mind Emily living in her attic at all. And the Lost Property Office was right next door to Jinks and O'Hare's house and workshop. Emily often peeked in to see what they were fixing, and sometimes O'Hare would let her help with small jobs such as unclogging mega-thunk pistons or replacing worn-out thunderspin sprockets.

On the particular morning when this story begins, Emily was woken up as usual by the silence, and lay in bed for a few moments trying to remember if it was a school day or not.

School days weren't really too bad, because Emily didn't have to go to an ordinary school. Like all the other kids who lived on Funfair Moon, she studied at the Learny-Go-Round, an educational roundabout designed by the famous scientist, Floomish Spoob. Professor Spoob had discovered that people always learn more when they are on the move (that is why travel broadens the mind, but nobody learns much while they are asleep). So on the Learny-Go-Round the pupils sat at desks which whirled around and around the central podium where the teacher stood. During the more difficult lessons they also went up and down, like the painted horses on a carousel.

This meant that some people got quite travel sick during double maths, but luckily Floomish Spoob had also worked out that too much education in one go was bad for the brain, so the

Learny-Go-Round was only open every other day. And since Emily remembered going yesterday, that meant that today was a day off, and she could do whatever she liked.

Yay!

She jumped out of bed, got dressed, and slid down the indoor slide which Jinks and O'Hare had installed as a way of getting quickly downstairs.

Jumping off in the kitchen, she poured herself a glass of glowberry juice, and made some toast. As soon as she had eaten the toast, drunk the juice and taken her plate and glass to the washing-up machine, she climbed out of the window and scampered across the yard to Jinks and O'Hare's house. It was a neat little house, with a workshop and tool store attached to the side, and a sign above the door which said:

JINKS & O'HARE
FUNFAIR REPAIR

Jinks and O'Hare were outside the workshop, loading up their aircar ready to whizz off and repair anything that needed repairing. Mr O'Hare was as hairy as his name suggested, and completely round; a big ball of fur with long furry arms and short furry legs sticking out and a bowler hat perched on the top. Mr Jinks wore a bowler hat too, but he was straight and thin. When they stood side by side they looked a bit like the number 10.

Jinks and O'Hare were Emily's heroes. She loved following them around the fair, helping them while they checked the rides and made sure everything stayed safe and fun. It was her ambition to join their team and become a funfair repair person just like them. Living above the Lost Property Office wasn't much of a claim to fame, not when all your friends' mums and dads ran roller coasters and roundabouts and wall-of-death ultrascooter stunt teams. But Jinks and O'Hare had just about the most important job on the whole moon, so when people said, 'What did you do after school yesterday?' it would be brilliant to be able to say, 'Oh, I was working with Jinks and O'Hare, we had to do some routine maintenance . . .' In Emily's dreams, that sign on the front of their house said:

JINKS&
O'HARE
AND EMILY
FUNFAIR REPAIR

The trouble was, Jinks and O'Hare didn't seem to understand how useful an almost-ten-year-old could be, and most of the time they wouldn't let her help.

Mr O'Hare gave Emily a big, furry smile when he saw her, but Mr Jinks just said, 'Ah, Emily,' in a shouldn't-you-be-at-school-little-hatchling? sort of voice.

'What's on your list today?' asked
Emily, trying to get a peek at Jinks's
clipboard, where he kept his list of things
which needed fixing around the fair.

Mr Jinks held the clipboard against his
chest so that she couldn't see. 'We have
all sorts of things to do,' he said. 'We
really must be going.'

O'Hare shrugged at him. O'Hare never
said much, but he was very good at
shrugging. Mrs Mimms always
said that one of O'Hare's
shrugs was worth a
thousand words.

This particular shrug was worth exactly five words, and they were: *Can't Emily come with us?*

Jinks shook his head firmly. Children embarrassed him. He could never think of what to say to them. 'Sorry,' he said, climbing into the car and starting the engine. He waved the clipboard. 'We have a lot of jobs to do, and they're all jobs for qualified repairmen, not small girls.'

O'Hare wiggled his eyebrows at Emily. He was very good at wiggling his eyebrows too, and she knew that this particular eyebrow-wiggle meant, *Sorry! Maybe another day . . .*

Then he climbed into the car too, Mr Jinks closed the domed glass lid over them both, and it went puttering out of the workshop and off into the funfair.

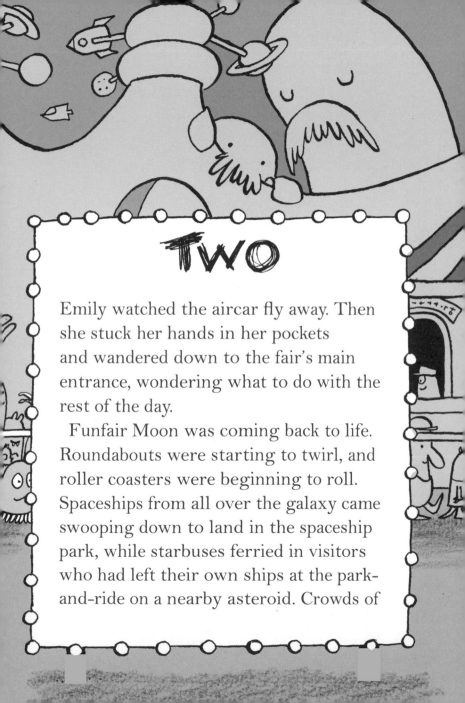

TWO

Emily watched the aircar fly away. Then she stuck her hands in her pockets and wandered down to the fair's main entrance, wondering what to do with the rest of the day.

Funfair Moon was coming back to life. Roundabouts were starting to twirl, and roller coasters were beginning to roll. Spaceships from all over the galaxy came swooping down to land in the spaceship park, while starbuses ferried in visitors who had left their own ships at the park-and-ride on a nearby asteroid. Crowds of

visitors were already pouring through
the turnstiles, all eager to try the rides.
Emily watched them, feeling a little
sorry for herself.

Suddenly a big shadow fell over her.
She looked up in surprise, and jumped
out of the way just as a big grey
spaceship came down out of the sky. It
was box-shaped, and its name seemed
to be *Official Spaceship RT 372/C*, which
Emily thought was the most boring

name for a
spaceship
she had
ever seen.
It touched
down
awkwardly.
One of its
landing legs
squashed
an I-Speak-
Your-Weight

machine, which said *'You weigh 7,224 tonnes, argh zzxxzx . . .'*

Emily watched with interest as a dull grey hatch opened in the spaceship's dull grey side. Out came a large hat with a small man underneath it.

'Excuse me,' said Emily, in her sternest voice. 'You can't park here!'

'Oh, yes I can,' smirked the small man.

Mrs Mimms came slithering out of her Lost Property Office with a lost hatbox clutched between her tentacles. 'Emily's right,' she said. 'That machine belongs in the car park! It is forbidden for visitors to park their spacecraft inside the funfair.'

'Not for me, it isn't,' said the man. He pulled out a little wallet and opened it to reveal a huge holographic badge with the words OFFICIAL FUNFAIR INSPECTOR revolving around it. 'I am Jeremy Moonbottom from the Galactic Council (Leisure and Entertainment

Sub-Committee). This is my assistant,
Miss Weebly.'

'I'm-very-pleased-to-meet-you,' said a
lady who had been hidden behind him
until then. She spoke very quickly and
quietly, blushing deep pink.

'But what are you here for?' asked Emily. 'Funfair Moon had its official health and safety inspection last month. We passed with flying colours. The inspector said this was the best run funfair she'd ever seen.'

'If it's so well run, you won't mind another inspection, will you?' asked Mr Moonbottom, looking around. 'I do like to drop in unannounced, so I can see what really goes on.'

'*Ooof,*' groaned the I-Speak-Your-Weight machine, which was still stuck under his spaceship. '*Gerrof, fatty!*'

'Aha!' said Mr Moonbottom, whirling round to stare at it. 'A defective slot machine! That's a black mark against Funfair Moon straight away. Make a note of that, Miss Weebly.'

'But that's not fair!' shouted Emily. 'You squashed that machine yourself!'

'Excuses, excuses,' said Mr Moonbottom. 'Mark it down, Miss

Weebly, and then we'll go and see how many other hazards and failures we can find.' He looked over his shoulder at Mrs Mimms as he started stalking off. 'Needless to say, if I'm not impressed, your whole fair will be closed down.'

Miss Weebly made a note on the clipboard she carried, then smiled vaguely at Emily and hurried after Mr Moonbottom.

Closed down? thought Emily. Up until he said that, she had just felt angry at the Funfair Inspector. Now she felt frightened, too. Could he really close down Funfair Moon? And if he did, where would everyone go? What would become of Mrs Mimms, and Jinks and O'Hare? What would become of Emily?

'I don't suppose it's anything to worry about,' said Mrs Mimms, when the Funfair Inspector and his assistant had gone. 'He seems a nasty piece of work,

but Funfair Moon has never failed an
inspection yet.'

'That's because of Jinks and O'Hare,'
said Emily, and she felt better already,
just thinking about them. 'They're
the best funfair repairers in the whole
galaxy. But I'd better go and find them.

We ought to let them know there's an inspector on the way.'

'I think Mr Jinks said they were going to be doing some work on the Space Twizzler this morning,' said Mrs Mimms. 'Apparently it's gone a bit wonky-woo.'

'Brilliant!' said Emily, and dashed off to find them.

'Have a nice morning!' called Mrs Mimms, waving with a couple of tentacles while she reached back into the Lost Property Office with another and carefully placed the hatbox on a high shelf.

She did not notice the hatbox open. Something black and spiny came out of it, like a sooty sea urchin. There were two white eyes among the spines, which blinked down at Mrs Mimms for a moment. Then, with a rustling noise like crumpled sweet wrappers, the strange creature vanished into the shadows at the back of the shelf.

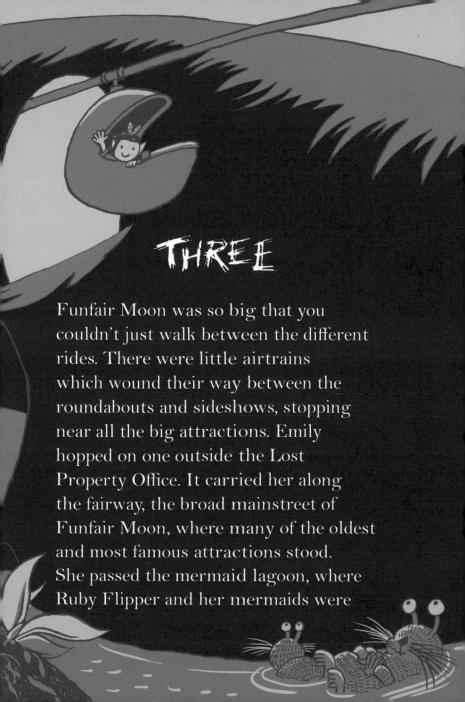

THREE

Funfair Moon was so big that you couldn't just walk between the different rides. There were little airtrains which wound their way between the roundabouts and sideshows, stopping near all the big attractions. Emily hopped on one outside the Lost Property Office. It carried her along the fairway, the broad mainstreet of Funfair Moon, where many of the oldest and most famous attractions stood. She passed the mermaid lagoon, where Ruby Flipper and her mermaids were

getting ready for the first synchronized swimming show of the day, and the lawnmower arena, where Burt Turbot and his Lawnmower Display Team were getting ready for the first synchronized strimming show of the day. She passed Peeploid's Astounding Seven Storey Merry-Go-Round and Fudge Shoppe, where Amy lived.

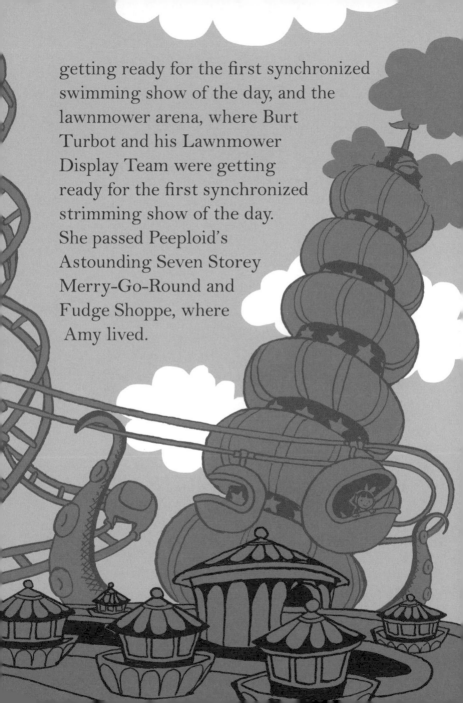

She wondered about hopping off there and seeing if Amy wanted to come with her, but she knew Amy would be helping her mum and dad get ready for the day ahead. At last the train stopped at the Space Twizzler.

The Space Twizzler was a giant helter-skelter, decorated with pictures of suns and moons and planets. That morning a rope was stretched across the entrance with an

OUT OF ORDER

sign dangling from it, but Emily ducked under it and ran over to her two friends, who were busy getting things out of their toolbox.

'Jinks!' shouted Emily. 'O'Hare!'

They turned and looked at her.

'Emily,' said Jinks, in an oh-dear-what-do-you-want? sort of way.

O'Hare just smiled another big, furry smile.

She told them about the funfair inspector.

'But that can't be right!' said Jinks. 'We only had an inspector round last month!'

'Well, there's another one now,' said Emily, 'and this one's a real meanie.' And she explained about the I-Speak-Your-Weight machine, and what Mr Moonbottom had said about closing down the funfair.

O'Hare looked at Jinks and gave a Meaningful Shrug.

'You are quite right, O'Hare,' said Jinks. 'We'd better get to the bottom of this trouble with the Space Twizzler before

this inspector comes snooping round. It wouldn't do for him to see it in this condition. That would not do at all.'

'What's gone wrong with it, then?' asked Emily, peering up at the Twizzler. It was a very tall helter-skelter—so tall that its top was hidden by low cloud. The slide went spiralling round it, up and up. It looked all right to Emily. She couldn't really think what would go wrong with a helter-skelter. Perhaps it had lost its slidiness?

'Don't you have school to go to, Emily?' Jinks asked hopefully.

'Not today,' Emily told him. 'Floomish Spoob says that it's very bad for children to have to go to school two days running.'

'Hmmph,' said Jinks, watching O'Hare adjust an adjustable spanner.

'Well, I'm sure you have a lot of other things you want to be doing . . .'

'Not really,' said Emily. 'I'm just going to watch you.'

She had learned that sometimes, if she watched Jinks and O'Hare work for long enough, Mr Jinks would get self-conscious and find something for her to do, like scraping the rust off an old dodgem car, or painting new gold twirly bits on the carousel horses, which was completely brilliant. She looked around for somewhere to sit, and decided that the slide itself looked comfiest. At the bottom of the slide a lot of the hairy mats which people slid down on had been scattered on the ground. Emily picked one up and dragged it over to the end of the slide. Jinks and O'Hare had opened the front of a big control box that stood near the ticket booth and they were peering worriedly inside. They didn't notice what Emily was doing until she was about to sit down on the mat. Then O'Hare looked up. He dropped his

tools and came running towards Emily,
waving his hairy arms.

'No!' shouted Jinks. 'Don't sit on the
slide! There's been a serious gravity
inversion . . .'

Emily was about to ask what a gravity
inversion was, but just then she found
out. Almost as soon as her bottom
landed on the mat, she began moving.
She wasn't sure what was happening at

first, but then, as the movement grew faster and faster, she understood. She was sliding *up* the Space Twizzler. That was what Jinks must have meant about the gravity thing, she thought, clutching the edge of the mat and squeaking in fright as it began to whirl its way up the enormous slide. The helter-skelter was working backwards!

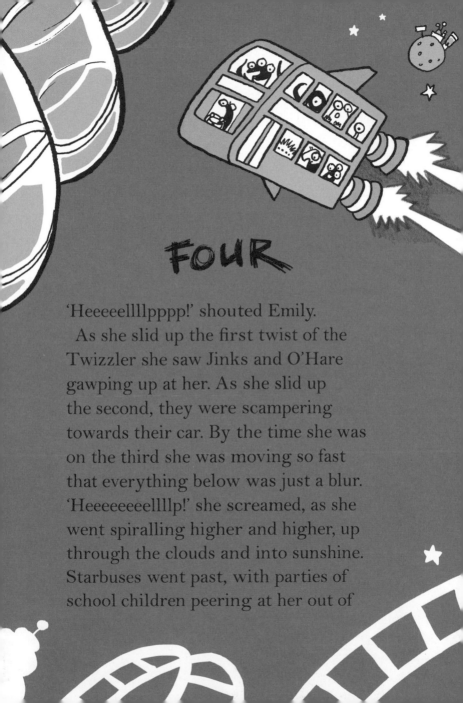

FOUR

'Heeeeellllpppp!' shouted Emily.

As she slid up the first twist of the Twizzler she saw Jinks and O'Hare gawping up at her. As she slid up the second, they were scampering towards their car. By the time she was on the third she was moving so fast that everything below was just a blur. 'Heeeeeeeellllp!' she screamed, as she went spiralling higher and higher, up through the clouds and into sunshine. Starbuses went past, with parties of school children peering at her out of

the windows as they descended towards
the spaceport. The Space Twizzler
was one of the best helter-skelters on
Funfair Moon, and Emily had always
loved sliding down it. But sliding *up* it
was no fun at all, because she couldn't
help worrying about what was going to
happen when she got to the top.

Luckily, the Twizzler wasn't one of
those helter-skelters which have a lid
on them, like a pepperpot. At the top of
the slide was a wide, open platform with
a handrail around it, where you could
stand and look out over the fair while
you waited for your turn.

Unluckily, Emily was going so fast
when she reached the top of the slide
that she kept going, shooting straight
over the handrail and out into the empty
air. As the top of the Space Twizzler
fell away below she thought she saw
something go scurrying across it—a
small, black, spiny something, like an

inky sea urchin. But she couldn't see it clearly, and a moment later she couldn't see it at all—the view of the fair spread out below her and the thought of the long drop to the ground make her squeeze her eyes tight shut.

And then, just as she was wondering how long it would take before she hit the ground, she hit something else instead. Something soft, furry, and unexpected. For a moment she thought she had collided with a passing cloud, but when she opened one eye and then the other she found that the thing she had hit was solid,

and very hairy. In fact, it was definitely O'Hare-y. The furry repairman was holding Emily tight in his big furry arms, and when she looked down she saw that he was standing on the roof of the little flying car, which Mr Jinks was driving.

Jinks twitched one eye-stalk so that he was looking straight up at her through the car's glass roof. 'Have you got her, Mr O'Hare?' he asked. 'Well, don't hang about out there admiring the view. Bring her inside and let's get back down to ground level.'

O'Hare opened a panel in the roof and lowered Emily gently down through it into the back seat.

'Next time someone tells you to stay away from a broken ride, young lady,' glowered Jinks, 'I hope you'll listen. The Space Twizzler started working backwards last night. The people who were sliding down it when it first went

wrong were all shot straight back up,
flew off the top, and landed in the candyfloss vats. That's where you would
have ended up if I hadn't had the quick-
thinking to fly the aircar up here and
position O'Hare ready to catch you.'

O'Hare poured himself down through
the roof and landed in the passenger
seat, giving Mr Jinks a hard stare, and a
shrug which said, *What do you mean, you
had the idea?*

'Well, all right, it was O'Hare's idea,'
admitted Jinks. 'But it was me who kept
us hovering in position. It took nerves
of steel.'

They both
gave Emily
a long,
severe
stare.

'Thank you,' said Emily, with what she hoped was a repentant expression. And she meant it. She thought they'd been very brave, flying up to save her like that. She would have hated to crash into a candyfloss vat. It would have been such a waste of candyfloss.

'Hmmph,' said Jinks, and started steering the car back down. 'Well, don't do it again. Now, Mr O'Hare, we need to get this Twizzler sorted out. The problem is in the control box. All our rides have their own gravity generator, since Funfair Moon is too small to have much gravity of its own. This one has been reversed somehow. I can't imagine how it happened. Or how we're going to sort it out.'

'Let me help!' said Emily eagerly.

'NO,' said Jinks. Mr O'Hare looked away and shrugged, and Emily slouched her own shoulders in frustration.

'I'm sorry, Emily,' Jinks went on, as

he steered the little car carefully down
to land at the foot of the Twizzler.
'This is a very serious problem, and we
can't have a little hatchling interfering,
sticking her fingers into live circuits and
getting tangled up in the gravity fields.
We need to get this Twizzler sorted out
before the Inspector comes . . .'

But they were too late. When the car
settled into the grass and Mr O'Hare
flipped the roof open, there was the
Funfair Inspector himself standing at
the entrance,
scowling at
the OUT OF
ORDER sign.

'What is going
on here?' he sniffed.
'Trouble with this
helter-skelter, is
there?'

'Certainly not!'
said Mr Jinks.

'We were just doing some routine checks, and we haven't had time to take the sign down.'

'I see,' said the Inspector. He nodded to Miss Weebly, who made a note on her clipboard. 'Very well. If the helter-skelter is in use, we'd better test it, hadn't we, Miss Weebly?'

'Oh, yes, Mr Moonbottom!' she twittered, and went hurrying through the entrance to the lift which carried people up to the top of the Twizzler.

'No!' shouted Jinks.

O'Hare ran after her. He overtook her, and stepped in front of the lift door, barring the way with his hairy arms spread wide.

'Whatever is the matter?' asked the Funfair Inspector.

O'Hare shrugged.

'Um . . .' said Jinks.

Emily could see that he needed rescuing. Mr Jinks was a terrible liar. He couldn't think of a thing to say. So she said something instead.

'You don't need to go up in the lift!' she said. 'This isn't a helter-skelter. It's a skelter-helter.'

'A skelter-helter?' asked Moonbottom.

'I'm not sure I've heard of one of those,' said Miss Weebly.

'It's exactly like a helter-skelter, only the other way round,' said Emily. She picked up a mat from the pile and handed it to Miss Weebly. 'Just sit down at the bottom of the slide on that.'

'Like this?' asked Miss Weebly, setting the mat down carefully and sitting. 'Well, how very odd, I . . . Ooooh!'

Jinks and O'Hare were already running to their aircar. Emily and Mr Moonbottom watched as Miss Weebly shot up the slide, going faster and faster, until she was just a blur.

'Wheeeeeeeee . . . !' she said.

'Hmmm,' said Mr Moonbottom.

A few seconds later, his assistant was back, carried safely to ground level by the aircar. She was rather flushed and her hair was standing up on end, but she seemed to have enjoyed herself. 'Wow!' she said. 'That was such fun! Can I have another go?'

'Really, Miss Weebly,' snapped Moonbottom. 'We're not here to enjoy ourselves. We have a great many other rides to inspect. Come on!'

He turned and stalked away towards the next ride, and Miss Weebly hurried after him.

Jinks slumped against the aircar, holding his head in his hands. 'This is dreadful! What bad luck! A surprise inspection on the very day that something goes seriously wrong!'

'Er, excuse me, Mr Jinks,' said someone who had been waiting nearby. It was Midge Flimsy, who went to school with Emily. Her mum and dad ran a hook-the-duck attraction on nearby Sideshow Hill. 'The Space Twizzler isn't the only thing that's gone seriously wrong! My dad sent me to find you. Our duck pond has sprung a leak!'

Mr O'Hare's hair stood on end, and
Mr Jinks turned green with worry.
(Actually he was green to start with,
but he turned a different shade of
green.) Emily could understand why
they were so alarmed. Since Funfair
Moon's visitors came from all over the
galaxy, it had to have stalls and rides in
all shapes and sizes to cater for different
types of aliens. Most people fitted all
right into human-sized rides, but for
those who didn't there were tiny
roundabouts and Ferris

wheels which looked like super-detailed toys, and gigantic ones which even ten-metre-tall Arcturan dung beetles and Blovarian ultra-titans could enjoy. The Flimsys' sideshow was designed for Blovarian children, whose huge hands were way too big to manage the bamboo poles which most people used to hook ordinary-sized plastic ducks at ordinary-sized sideshows. The poles on Bob's stall were made from old telegraph poles, and his giant customers used them to hook giant ducks out of a huge tank of water. Looking uphill between the sweet stalls and coconut shies, Emily could see the tank perched on the summit. Midge's mum and dad were frantically trying to plug a little hole in its side, from which a long jet of water was shooting out. As Emily watched, another hole opened, and then another . . .

'If that tank splits, it will flood this whole part of the fair!' shouted Jinks,

running towards the aircar. 'We'll be
waist-deep in water and giant rubber
ducks! Quick, O'Hare! We need to get up
there!'

'Can I come?' Emily started to say.
She thought they might not mind her
tagging along after she had handled
the Funfair Inspector so well.
But Mr O'Hare
looked

down at
her and firmly
shook his head. Then
he grabbed his toolbox
and jumped into the car
beside Jinks. The car took
off and went speeding
towards the hilltop, with
Midge hurrying along in
its shadow.

Emily looked glumly
after them, wondering
how many more years
she would have to spend
Growing Up before Jinks
would let her fix something.
How was she supposed to
get any practice, if they
never let her help?

Just then, someone
else came
running
up.

It was the owner of Funfair Moon's famous ghost train. He was a plump alien with two heads, and both of them were called Stan. 'Are Jinks and O'Hare here?' he panted. 'I need their help! Something's gone wrong with my ghost train. People are saying there aren't any ghosts in it! They're asking for their money back!'

'No ghosts?' asked Emily. That sounded impossible. She'd never been inside the ghost train herself, because it sounded really scary. Everyone knew it was the most haunted ghost train in the Known Galaxy. It was simply stuffed with ghosts.

'I don't know what can have happened!' Stan wailed. 'I need Jinks and O'Hare to take a look around inside . . .'

'Well, they're rather busy at the moment,' said Emily, and pointed up the hill, where her friends were trying to patch the duck tank. Just then, a whole section of the tank's side gave way, letting out a gush of water and a huge yellow duck which knocked Jinks off his feet and went rolling downhill to smash into a coconut shy.

'I'll tell them about the ghost train as soon as they're finished up there,' Emily promised.

Stan looked unhappy. 'Well, I just hope they can come and sort my spooks out soon. I've heard there's a Funfair Inspector going round. If he finds I'm running a ghost train with no ghosts there'll be all kinds of trouble. It's probably against all the regulations . . .'

Emily saw his point. 'I tell you what,' she said, in her best Taking Charge voice. 'I'll come and look at your ghost train for you.'

'You?' asked Stan, looking surprised and doubtful (it's easy to do two expressions at once if you've got two heads).

'Yes,' explained Emily. 'I'm Jinks and O'Hare's assistant. I'm part of their team. They're teaching me everything they know.'

'Really?' said Stan, both faces looking doubtful now. But he could tell that Jinks and O'Hare were going to be busy with the duck tank for a while, so he let Emily take his hand and lead him back towards the ghost train.

Funfair Moon was filling up with happy visitors. Emily hoped the Funfair Inspector was mingling with the crowds on the fairway and noticing all their happy smiles and the fun that they were having. But ahead, a grey cloud loomed in the sky. It was always there, that cloud: it was the tethered storm that hung above the ghost train.

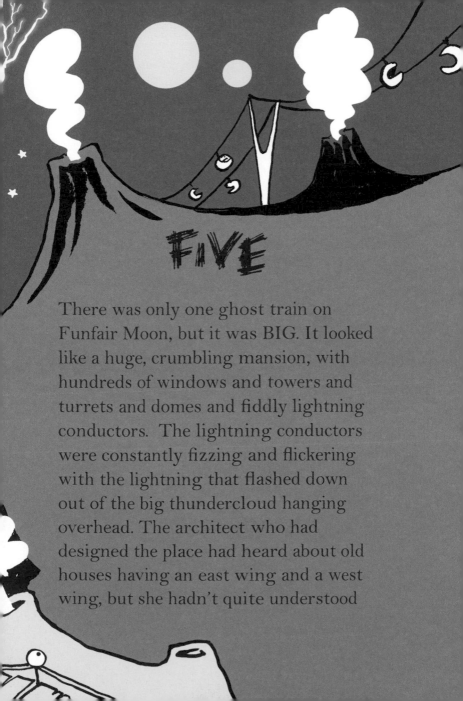

FIVE

There was only one ghost train on Funfair Moon, but it was BIG. It looked like a huge, crumbling mansion, with hundreds of windows and towers and turrets and domes and fiddly lightning conductors. The lightning conductors were constantly fizzing and flickering with the lightning that flashed down out of the big thundercloud hanging overhead. The architect who had designed the place had heard about old houses having an east wing and a west wing, but she hadn't quite understood

what that meant, so she had given this
house actual wings: they were huge and
bat-like and they stuck out of the roof
and flapped slowly all the time. That
was what kept the thundercloud slowly
turning, like the froth on a well-stirred
cup of coffee.

Usually there was a line of little
railway pods going in at one end of
the ghost train, full of excited kids
blowing raspberries and laughing and
saying they weren't scared because
there was No Such Thing As Ghosts.
Usually there was another line of little
pods coming out the other end, full of
quivering kids too scared to speak, with
chattering teeth, and hair that stood
on end as if they'd been electrified by
fright. Today there were no pods going
in at all, and the few people coming out
didn't look scared, just bored. Some of
them came over to complain when they
saw Stan and Emily. 'That wasn't very

scary!' they said. 'I never saw so much as a whisker of a ghost! Not a phantom sausage. We want our money back!'

'You see the trouble?' said Stan. 'I don't know what's wrong. My ghosts are professionals, they've never let us down before. I presume you have a special ghost detector with you?'

Emily hadn't. She wasn't even sure if Jinks and O'Hare carried such things. She said, 'I'll have a look inside, and then I can report back to Jinks and O'Hare.'

Stan helped her into one of the ghost train pods. She was still feeling a bit

nervous about riding the ghost train, but at least the pod was comfortable, like a little open-topped car with squishy seats. It was powered by the electricity which came down the lightning conductors from the storm cloud overhead. Lit up by the flashes of lightning, the haunted mansion looked scarier than ever. Emily started to wonder if this was really a good idea. She turned to tell Stan that she had decided to wait for Jinks and O'Hare after all—but Stan had already gone back to his control kiosk!

He threw a lever and spooky music started playing as the pod began to move.

There was no turning back now, thought Emily—not without looking like a complete scaredy cat. She held on

tightly to the arm-rests of her seat. The
pod trundled and squeaked along the
rails, and went into the haunted house
through an arched opening
where tickly curtains of
cobweb hung.

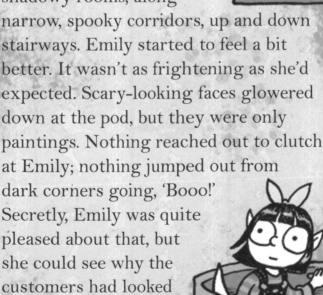

The rails which the pod
rolled on ran through
shadowy rooms, along
narrow, spooky corridors, up and down
stairways. Emily started to feel a bit
better. It wasn't as frightening as she'd
expected. Scary-looking faces glowered
down at the pod, but they were only
paintings. Nothing reached out to clutch
at Emily; nothing jumped out from
dark corners going, 'Booo!'
Secretly, Emily was quite
pleased about that, but
she could see why the
customers had looked
so disappointed.

TRUNDLE SQUEAK

'Not a ghost in sight!' she said to herself.

The pod banged through big double doors into a huge room filled with potted plants and creepy suits of armour. In the shadows, Emily thought she saw something move. She leaned out of the pod for a better look, but just then it jolted over a hump in the track.

'Eek!' said Emily, tumbling out.

By the time she had picked herself up and brushed the dust off, the pod was vanishing through another set of doors. She ran after it, but the doors had locked themselves.

'Bother!' said Emily. She tried not to feel too scared, all alone in the huge, dark room.

Or perhaps not quite all alone . . . Out of the corner of her eye, she glimpsed a movement.

'Hello?' she said nervously.

'Hello,' said a small voice coming from

behind a rubber plant. It sounded even more nervous than hers did. 'Who are you?' it asked.

'I'm Emily,' said Emily. 'Who are you?'

'I'm a ghost,' said the voice.

Emily wondered if she should be frightened, but the ghost didn't sound very frightening, and when it drifted out from behind the rubber plant it didn't look very frightening either. It was a small ghost, about the size of a pillow case, and it was holding a cuddly penguin.

'My name's See-through George,' it said.

'Are you really a ghost?' asked Emily. 'You're not very scary . . .'

'I'm only little,' said See-through George. 'I haven't really got the hang of it yet. You should see my mum and dad, and my big brother, and Uncle Reggie, and Headless Maude. They'd scare the pants off you!'

'Where are they, then?' asked Emily (although she didn't really want her pants scared off).

'They're HIDING,' said See-through George. 'I was hiding, too. But then I realized I'd left Penguin out here, so I came to get him.'

'What, hiding so you can jump out at people with bloodcurdling screams?' asked Emily.

'No,' said the ghost. 'Hiding because we're scared!'

'What are ghosts scared of?'

'Rustlers!' said See-through George. 'They're black and spiky! They come up through the floor and they rustle in the shadows . . .'

That reminded Emily of something, but before she could remember what, there was a sudden rustling sound from the far end of the room. The little ghost quivered with fright and pressed close to Emily. 'Hear that?' it whispered. 'This place is HAUNTED!'

Emily was frightened too, but she knew that she mustn't let the little ghost know that, so she looked as brave as she could, and took hold of his hand. It was like holding a handful of smoke.

'It's all right, See-through George,' she said. 'I'm working with Jinks and O'Hare, and they can sort out any problem. Listen! I can hear a pod coming. Maybe it's Stan, coming to look for me! He might even have Jinks and O'Hare with him. They'll know what to do.'

The doors banged open, and the pod appeared. But as the beam from its headlamp swept across the room and reflected from the dusty mirrors on the

walls, Emily saw that it wasn't Stan riding in it. It was Mr Moonbottom and Miss Weebly.

'Honestly!' the Funfair Inspector was saying. 'Not a single spook! Disgraceful! Make a note of that, Miss Weebly: Ghost Train—V. Disappointing . . .'

Emily pulled See-through George back into the shadows with her as the pod rumbled past and vanished through the far doors.

'Oh no!' she said, as the pod's noise faded. 'This is bad! That's Mr Moon-bottom, the Funfair Inspector. He's trying to close down Funfair Moon!'

'What are we going to do?' asked See-through George.

Emily thought for a moment. 'Can we go and get your mum and dad and Uncle Thingy and Headless Whatshername?'

'They're right up in the attic,' said See-through George. 'They're too scared to come out!'

'Right, then we're going to have to scare Mr Moonbottom ourselves,' Emily decided. 'He just needs one really good fright; he can't call the ghost train "V. Disappointing" then. Can we get round in front of his pod?'

See-through George nodded. 'Yes. There's a secret short cut from here to the dining room. The dining room is the last room the pods go through on their way to the exit. But what about all the Rustlers?'

'I don't believe there's any such thing,' said Emily. 'I think you've all been letting your imaginations run away with you. Those noises you heard were probably just some dropped sweet wrappers rustling about in a draught. Now, how can I get into one of these suits of armour?'

But it turned out that the suits of armour were much too big for her, and much too complicated to climb into quickly. So she just grabbed a helmet from one of them and hurried after See-through George. There was a tiny door at the far end of the room. It was so small, and so deep in shadows, that Emily wouldn't have noticed it, but luckily there were helpful signs pointing to it:

She pushed the
door open and
See-through
George brushed
past her
and floated
ahead of
her down
a cobwebby
secret corridor.

They came out on a sort of
balcony—See-through George called
it a 'gallery'—overlooking a huge
dining room. Candles flickered in big
chandeliers above a table shrouded
in more cobwebs. The rail which
carried the ghost train pods ran in
a loop right around the table, and it
was already starting to thrum and
tremble as Mr Moonbottom's
pod approached.

'As soon as it comes through the doors,' whispered Emily, 'we need to start waving our arms and shouting, 'Booo!' and 'Woooo!' and things. You probably know more about it than I do, being a ghost and everything. Do you think you'd be scarier if you weren't carrying a cuddly penguin?'

See-through George just clutched his penguin more tightly.

'I'll tell you what,' said Emily, 'I'll look after him for you, and you can have him back after we've done the scary bit.' She took the toy, but unfortunately she didn't have any pockets big enough for it, so she opened the visor of her helmet and popped it inside—the helmet was quite roomy, so there was plenty of room for a cuddly penguin between her head and the top of the visor—it worked like padding, and made the helmet much more comfortable.

Just then the dining room doors

opened, and the pod came humming in.
'Oh, Funfair Moon is going to fail its
inspection at this rate!' Mr Moonbottom
was saying. He sounded rather pleased
about it. 'We shall have to shut the
whole place down!'

'Booooo!' yelled Emily, up in the
gallery.

'WooooOOOOooo!' wailed the little
ghost. But his voice wasn't very loud,
and Emily's voice was muffled by the
penguin, which had chosen that moment
to flop down between her face and the
visor. Mr Moonbottom and Miss Weebly
didn't so much as
look up at the
gallery.
They
hadn't
heard the
blood-
curdling
cries!

Something had, though. In the shadows at the far end of the gallery spiky black shapes moved and rustled. They reminded Emily of the spiny creature she had seen scurrying across the top of the helter-skelter as she shot over the handrail.

'Rustlers!' squeaked See-through George, wrapping his arms around Emily's waist. She stepped backwards, and the weight of the big helmet on her head made her overbalance. She crashed through the balcony railing, with the frightened ghost still clinging tightly to her. Luckily, she caught hold of one of the chandeliers as she fell, and from there it was just a short drop to the table. But the table wasn't meant to be stood on—not by anyone who wasn't a ghost, anyway. It collapsed with a huge crash, and Emily tumbled off straight into the path of the oncoming pod.

'Aaaaargh!' screamed Mr Moonbottom
and Miss Weebly, as See-through
George whirled over their heads.
'Eeeeek!' they shrieked, as the dust from
the collapsing table cleared to reveal an
awful figure on the tracks ahead.

75

It swung its huge armoured head to look at them and said, 'I can't see a thing through this penguin . . .' Then it fumbled with the helmet, its visor popped open, and a weird bird-like face

stared out at them.

'Eeeeeeek!' shrieked Mr Moonbottom and Miss Weebly, grabbing hold of each other. 'Aaiiiiieeeee!' they screeched.

'Ghosts! Monsters! A Haunted Penguin!'

The apparition jumped out of the way, and the pod carried them through the door at the far end of the dining room and out through cobwebs into the open air. Emily pulled the helmet off and looked about. There was no sign of the spiky things which had moved in the shadows. Just See-through George, hugging his penguin and doing a little dance. 'We scared them!' he said. 'Did you see how scared they were, Emily?

That was brilliant!'

Emily checked again for signs of the rustling things, and decided it was safe to leave See-through George on his own for a bit. She said, 'Listen, you go straight back upstairs to your family, all right?'

'OK Emily,' said the ghost, grinning from ear to see-through ear. He shot across the room and vanished through a side-door marked STAFF ONLY, while Emily followed the tracks through the double doors, pushed another curtain of cobwebs aside, and stepped out blinking into the daylight.

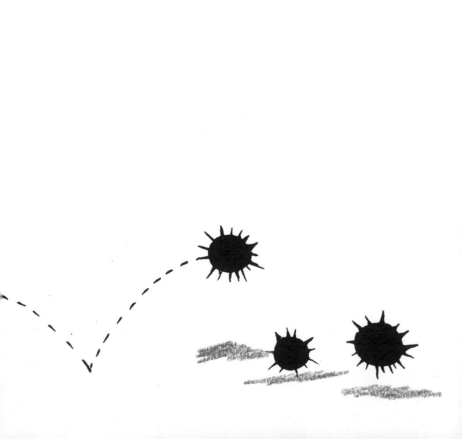

SIX

Funfair Moon was filling up fast. There were people everywhere, and all the rides were busy. The sky was full of flying pleasure boats and, higher up, big spaceships waiting for a parking space. Over the loudspeakers a cheery voice announced, 'Welcome to Funfair Moon! Among our visitors today, a party of cub scouts from the Foxfur Nebula! A whole wandering wood of tree-people from Grobag 12! And a star cruiser full of Space Commandos from the Darkvoids of Quorn! Yes, everyone comes to share

the fun here on Funfair Moon!'

But to anyone who knew the sights and sounds of the great funfair—and NOBODY knew those sights and sounds better than Emily—there were definite signs that something odd was happening today. The music from the carousels sounded wonky and out-of-tune, and on the main fairway Peeploid's Seven Storey Merry-Go-Round and Fudge Shoppe was spinning much faster than usual, with little wisps of smoke seeping from it.

Luckily, Mr Moonbottom didn't seem to have noticed. He and Miss

 Weebly were clambering out of their ghost train car at the end of the ride, looking white and shaken.

'It was a long build-up,' Miss Weebly was saying, 'but it was certainly scary in the end!'

'I'm not so sure, Miss Weebly,' said the Funfair Inspector, straightening his hat and brushing cobwebs off his briefcase. 'I'm not sure it can be called a "ghost train" when it features only one ghost and that strange armoured penguin thing . . .'

They hadn't noticed Emily. She hurried past them to the kiosk.

'There you are!' said Stan. 'I was getting worried. I was going to come in and look for you, but then that Inspector turned up. He's not very nice, is he? He reminds me of a customer we had last week, a right grumpy sort, complaining about everything . . .'

'Are Jinks and O'Hare here yet?' Emily asked.

Stan shook his heads. 'They won't be for a while, either. I've heard they've drained the duck tank, but now there's

another emergency going on over at Peeploid's Merry-Go-Round and Fudge Shoppe. Young Amy Peeploid came running over to tell me about it. The brakes have failed! The whole ride is spinning out of control. If Jinks and O'Hare can't stop it soon, it will . . .'

A huge **BOOM** echoed across the fair, and it started raining fudge. Emily gasped, and looked towards the fairway. Where the Peeploids' ride had stood there was just a spreading cloud of purple smoke.

Out of the smoke, big chunks of fudge were hurtling.

'Oh no!' Emily whispered, hoping that none of her friends had been on the Merry-Go-Round when it blew up. 'It's a fudge-tastrophe!'

Mr Moonbottom came hurrying over. 'Whatever was that din?' he asked. 'It registered 150 decibels on my noise-o-meter. Let me tell you about the Galactic Council's noise regulations . . .'

But Emily and Stan never did hear about the noise regulations, because at that moment a large cardboard box labelled PEEPLOID'S DELICIOUS FUDGE (VANILLA) came whooshing out of the sky and landed with a loud thud on Mr Moonbottom's head. He frowned, dropped his briefcase, and fell over.

'Oh dear!' twittered Miss Weebly, running over to him. 'He's out cold! I'm pretty sure that's a health and safety violation . . . Do you always throw fudge about like that?'

'Oh yes!' said Emily, hoping that Miss Weebly wouldn't notice the wreckage of the Merry-Go-Round and Fudge Shoppe, still feebly spinning in the distance as the smoke cleared. 'The Fudge Display is a very popular feature. It happens every day, and twice at weekends. Only usually they take the fudge out of the boxes first.' She started to pick up the things which had fallen out of Mr Moonbottom's briefcase when he dropped it. Some sandwiches wrapped in cling film, a few brochures from other funfairs, and a small book. It was the kind of book that you find in pet shops, and it was called, *How to Keep and Care for your Peladorian Puffball.*

There were pictures inside of round, fluffy creatures so fluffy and cuddly-looking that it made Emily wonder if she had been wrong about Mr Moonbottom. Surely someone who kept such cute pets couldn't be all bad?

'We'd better put him somewhere comfortable,' she said.

'Yes, probably best he's out of it,' said Stan, emerging from his kiosk. 'Everything's going wrong today. Maybe when he comes to, we'll be able to make him think it was all a dream.'

'We'll take him to the Lost Property Office,' said Emily. 'Mrs Mimms will look after him. She knows first aid, and she has a nice comfy sofa we can put him on. Comfy sofas are good for people who've been knocked out by fudge.'

So Stan put a notice on the window of his kiosk saying,

CLOSED FOR
GHOSTLY
TEA-BREAK

BACK SOON

Then he fetched his little hovertruck,
and Emily helped him and Miss
Weebly load the unconscious Funfair
Inspector onto the back of it. Miss
Weebly bought the fudge along, too.
'It seems a pity to waste it,' she said,
and they all ate fudge as Stan drove

them through the fair towards the Lost Property Office. Miss Weebly seemed quite nice—she said it was her first day on the job, and how excited she had been when Mr Moonbottom said they were going to Funfair Moon. 'But he's very strict, isn't he?' she said, between mouthfuls of fudge. 'I became a Funfair Inspector because I love funfairs, but Mr Moonbottom seems to hate them. He's always finding fault with them, and closing them down . . .'

'Oh, look over there!' said Emily, pointing out of the left-hand window so that Miss Weebly wouldn't see the cranes lifting

giant ducks out of the tank on Sideshow
Hill, which had just come into sight
on the right. A few moments later she
had to make Miss Weebly look out of
the right window to avoid the view of
the wrecked Merry-Go-Round on the
fairway. People were milling about at the
bottom of it, happily picking up bits of
scorched fudge. Emily was relieved to
see the Peeploids and Jinks and O'Hare
among the crowd. They were looking a
bit more fudge-splattered than usual, but
basically all right.

There was another crowd at the Lost
Property Office. That was unusual,
too—most days, people only arrived
in ones or twos. Today, the queue was
spilling out of the doors, which made
it quite difficult for Miss Weebly and
Stan to carry Mr Moonbottom inside.
But Emily was used to slithering her
way through fairground crowds. She
wove her way to the front, where a very

embarrassed Mrs Mimms was trying to deal with about thirty complaints at once.

'This isn't my hat!'

'That's not my jetpack!'

'Where are our spoons?' demanded a Poglite space captain, beating his tentacles on the counter top while all his crew bounced up and down in their chimney-pot spacesuits shouting, 'Spoons! Spoons! Spoons!'

'I'm so sorry, so sorry!' poor Mrs Mimms kept saying, blushing every colour of the rainbow as she rummaged among the shelves of coats and hats and bags, trying to reunite angry customers with their belongings. 'Oh, Emily,' she said, spotting Emily peering over the counter, 'something dreadful has happened! I've never known so much lost property in one day! Things have been getting lost and mislaid all morning, and people are handing them in almost as fast as I can label them. And now the owners have started turning up to claim them, and I can't find them! Someone comes in asking for a lost bobble hat and I check my list and see Bobble Hat— Number 79—but when I fetch Number 79 it isn't a bobble hat, it's a pair of skis or a cement mixer. Somehow all the labels have got mixed up! You haven't touched them, have you dear?'

Emily shook her head. 'I've got an injured Funfair Inspector. Is it all right if we put him in the front room?'

'Of course, dear,' said Mrs Mimms absent-mindedly, reaching behind her for a teddy bear and coming back with a marble statuette of Floomish Spoob.

Suddenly a huge, booming voice cut through the din. It sounded as dark as space, and so commanding that everyone fell quiet at once, and drew aside to let the owner of the voice stride up to the counter. He loomed over them.

'Is this the place where lost things are brought?' he demanded.

'Y-yes, sir,' said Mrs Mimms.

'I have lost my son.'

'Your son? Well, a lost child is not technically lost property, sir, I think you need to . . .'

'SILENCE!'

roared the stranger. 'I am Lord Krull,

Commander of the Black Space Fleet, Conqueror of Worlds, Supreme Ruler of the Darkvoids of Quorn. Star systems tremble at my very name. But my wife's gone to her sister's for the weekend and she left me in charge of our little boy. So I thought I'd bring him to your Funfair Moon.

I'm told children enjoy this thing you call "fun".'

'Yes, we do,' said Emily.

'SILENCE!'

bellowed Lord Krull. 'Unfortunately, I got rather dizzy on the Learny-Go-Round.'

'But the Learny-Go-Round isn't a ride,' said Emily. 'It's our school . . .'

'I was told it would be educational,' said Lord Krull. 'But it went a bit faster than I was expecting.'

'. . . and it isn't even open today!' said Emily.

'While I was recovering, my lad must have wandered off. I asked those black, spiny creatures who were operating the ride if they saw which way he went, but they just rustled at me.'

'What black, spiny creatures?' asked Emily. Some of her teachers were pretty odd-looking, but none of them was black and spiny, and she couldn't think why they'd be operating the Learny-Go-Round when it wasn't a school day.

Lord Krull wasn't listening. 'I've been looking everywhere,' he said. 'I need you to FIND HIM. NOW! Or shall I order my Space Commandos to tear your puny fair to pieces?'

'Oh,' said Mrs Mimms, getting flustered and tying her tentacles in knots. 'Oh dear, no—what is the little lad's name, your lordshipness, sir?'

99

'He is Krull-va, son of Krull. But he prefers to be called Colin.'

'Colin?'

'It's a phase he's going through.'

Mrs Mimms fumbled about under the counter and came up with a big microphone connected to the fair's loudspeaker system. While she was trying to turn it on, Emily pushed past Lord Krull and ran outside. Jinks and O'Hare needed to hear about this. As she dashed towards the fairway she heard Mrs Mimms's voice crackling out of the loudspeakers, saying, 'Hello? Is this thing on? Testing, testing . . . Oh—This is a Lost Child Alert. Will Colin please make his way to the Lost Property Office: will Colin, Son of Krull, please come to the Lost Property Office . . .'

SEVEN

A big  sign had been stuck on the ticket booth outside Peeploid's Seven Storey Merry-Go-Round And Fudge Shoppe, but it wasn't really needed. You could tell the ride was out of order by the way it had turned into a big heap of wreckage with purple smoke pouring out of it. The Peeploids were standing glumly beside it, covered in fudge. There was no sign of the funfair repairmen though.

'Where are Jinks and O'Hare?' panted

Emily, running to where Amy Peeploid stood. 'They had to go,' said Amy. 'Something's gone wrong with the candyfloss stall.' 'What can go wrong with candyfloss?' asked Emily.

Across the fairground echoed an angry bellow, like a bad-tempered gorilla with its head stuck in a dustbin. She looked around. Beyond the Terror Mountain roller coaster something huge and pink and candyflossy was lumbering about.

A train was just passing, so Emily jumped aboard. At the entrance to Terror Mountain she found Jinks and O'Hare. They were carrying their toolboxes, and climbing into one of the roller coaster cars.

'Mr Jinks!' she shouted, squirming through the turnstile and hurrying over to them.

'Emily!' said Jinks. 'I'm sorry, we don't have time to talk. There's five hundred tons of angry candyfloss on the rampage on the far side of this roller coaster, and we have to stop it before that Funfair Inspector notices.'

'He won't!' said Emily. 'He got bludgeoned by some fudge. I suppose you could say he got *fudgeoned*. It was vanilla flavour. He's at the Lost Property Office. It's complete chaos there . . .'

'It's just one thing after another today,' Jinks complained. 'You'd best hurry back to the Lost Property Office and help Mrs Mimms.'

'But I think I know what the problem is!' said Emily.

Jinks and O'Hare looked doubtful. Their roller coaster car was already starting to edge forwards, and Jinks

sighed heavily. 'Jump in!' he told Emily.
'You can explain on the way . . .'

'Yessss!' thought Emily, as O'Hare

reached out a hairy arm to help her
scramble aboard, and she sat down
between them feeling very important
while Jinks helped her fasten the chunky
safety belt around herself.

Terror Mountain was an actual
mountain, one of the highest on Funfair

Moon. The people who had built the
roller coaster had sculpted it, making
the peaks pointier, levelling pathways
for the roller coaster rails to run up,
poking holes through crags and cliff
faces. The roller coaster looped through
it and around it like a mad marble
run, swooping through caverns,
rushing under waterfalls,
climbing rickety-looking
bridges up to the sharp peaks
and plummeting down the
other side.

Usually, one of the noisiest
noises on Funfair Moon was
the screams of the Terror

Mountain passengers, but today Jinks and O'Hare and Emily were the only ones riding it.

'All the candyfloss in the candyfloss vats has come alive somehow,' said Jinks, as their car climbed slowly up the first steep section of the ride. 'It's angry, too. It smashed the candyfloss stall to pieces, and went stomping off to look for other things to smash. As far as we can tell, it's heading for Terror Mountain. I've never known a day like this on Funfair Moon. So if you really know what's causing all these accidents . . .'

'I don't think they are accidents,' said Emily.

'What do you mean?'

'I mean that . . .' said Emily, and then went 'Eeeeeeeeeeeeeeeekkkkk!' for a few seconds as the roller coaster plunged down a vertical section into a deep cave.

'. . . I mean that I think someone's doing all this deliberately,' she went on, as the car went weaving speedily between the stalactites and stalagmites. 'When I was on the Space Twizzler I saw a black spiny creature rustling about up there. The ghosts in the Ghost Train have been scared away by more of them. And Lord Krull said when his son went missing there were black spiny creatures running the Learny-Go-Round, but it was meant to be closed today. These spiny blighters must have snuck in and set it working just so they could kidnap Lord Krull's Colin.'

'Lord Krull is here?' asked Jinks. 'His son is missing?'

'Yes, and he's awfully cross about it. If Colin doesn't show up he says he's going to unleash his Space Commandos and tear our puny fair to pieces.'

'Oh, that's all we need,' grumbled Jinks, blinking as the car shot out into daylight again and started spiralling up towards an impossibly pointy peak. Below them, a huge, pink, fluffy shape was clambering through the lower levels of the roller coaster, growling and bellowing. Who would have thought candyfloss would be so bad tempered, thought Emily.

'What is it so angry about?' she asked.

'You know how too much sugar can make you hyper and bad tempered?' asked Jinks. 'Well, the candyfloss creature is made of sugar. It's on a gigantic sugar-rush. It needs to get some greens in its diet.'

The candyfloss monster seemed to understand this in its primitive way. It was snatching up handfuls of the trees which grew on the lower slopes of Terror Mountain and cramming them into its pink cave of a mouth. But it was also eating rocks, and the big neon sign

that said 'Terror Mountain', and Emily
didn't think those were going to do it
much good. She said, 'I bet one of those
spiky creatures has been meddling with
the candyfloss vats as well . . .'

O'Hare shrugged a shrug which meant,
But why?

'Who are they?' asked Jinks. 'Why

would they want to sabotage our funfair?'

'I don't know,' said Emily. 'But See-through George—he's this ghost I made friends with—he said they came up through the floor of the ghost train.'

'Maybe they're using the old tunnels under the fair to move around,' mused Jinks. Then they all went, 'Aaaaaaaaaaaaaaaaaaaaaaargh!' as the roller coaster reached the top of the mountain and dropped several hundred metres, straight down.

The candyfloss monster heard them. It looked up, and its sticky pink face creased into an angry frown. It started scrambling through the loops and twirls of track, aiming to cut the car off when it reached the bottom of the drop.

In the car, Emily and O'Hare felt their hair dragged backwards by the force of the wind as they sped down towards the waiting monster. Jinks didn't have any hair, but his eyestalks were blown backwards. Emily couldn't understand how the repairmen managed to keep their hats on, but they did. Jinks reached into his toolbox and pulled out a gun.

'You're going to shoot it?' asked Emily, feeling a bit sorry for the candyfloss monster.

'Just tranquillizer darts,' said Jinks. 'We haven't had to use them since the

Rigellian Megawhale in the Aqua park evolved legs and started eating all the swing boats. That was before your time, young Emily . . .'

The candyfloss monster had reached the section of track which they were whizzing down. It glooped itself around it, reaching out with huge pink hands as the car came rushing towards it.

Jinks threw the tranquillizer gun to O'Hare and said, 'Remember, short, controlled bursts . . .'

O'Hare closed one eye and took careful aim, though Emily didn't really see why he needed to, since they were so close now, and the monster was so big, that he couldn't really miss.

Phut phut phut phut! went the gun.

The monster lunged at them. A huge pink hand closed round the car and ripped it off the tracks. They were raised high into the air, above the angry creature's roaring mouth. Then the roar

turned into a
yawn, the huge,
sticky fingers
lost their grip,

and the car dropped like a stone.

'Eeeeek!' screamed Emily.

Everything went pink.

When she managed to scrape the
candyfloss out of her eyes she found
that the car was lying on its side on the
monster's chest. The monster was lying
next to the roller coaster track, snoring
gently.

Jinks undid Emily's safety belt and
helped her out. They climbed down the
monster's sleeping side to the ground.

'Everyone all right?' asked Jinks.
'Right, we need to get back to the ghost
train and see if we can find out who
these spiny critters are, and what they
want.'

EIGHT

At the Terror Mountain exit, O'Hare passed his tranquillizer gun to the worried staff.

'The candyfloss creature will sleep for a few hours,' said Jinks. 'Hopefully it'll be in a better mood when it wakes up. If not, just tranquillize it again.'

A train clattered past, filled with happy cub scouts on their way to the boating lake. Jinks flagged it down. 'Can you drop us off at the ghost train?'

'Not in that state,' said the driver. 'You're a mass of candyfloss. You'll get your sticky fingers all over my nice clean seats.'

'But this is an emergency!' shouted Jinks. He shook his fist at the train as it breezed off. 'Idiot!'

O'Hare tugged at his sleeve and pointed. Not far off was a dodgem car arena. Dozens of the little cars, which looked like coloured metal baby shoes, were zooming about and slamming into one another. In most funfairs, the dodgems were powered by electric cables in the roof, but on Funfair Moon they had their own engines; they could go anywhere.

O'Hare led the way, and Jinks and

Emily followed him. There were some empty dodgems parked up at the edge of the arena, and they each climbed into one. Jinks's dodgem was immediately crashed into by a dodgem full of cheering students from Alpha Centauri. 'Stop it!' he shouted. 'I'm on official business, I am! Stop it I say! Ooof!'

The students were having too much fun ramming Jinks's car to take any notice of what he was shouting. O'Hare shrugged at Emily. Then he put his foot down and rammed the students' car so hard that it went skittering right across the arena, where it was set upon by some other dodgems.

'Thank you, O'Hare,' said Jinks, straightening his bowler. Then he turned his dodgem around and crashed out through the low wall which ran around the arena, bouncing down onto the grass outside. O'Hare and Emily drove out after him. 'We're on official business, we are!' shouted Emily over her shoulder when the dodgem man came running after them to ask what the big idea was.

They quickly left him behind. The dodgem cars were speedy and easy to steer. The little convoy whisked through the crowds, Jinks in the lead, sounding his horn in a loud, official way. They were just passing the teacups ride when a bulky figure in battle armour barged out in front of them.

'Out of the way!' shouted Jinks, but the figure didn't move. It didn't even move when Jinks's dodgem car bashed into it. Jinks stopped the car, and O'Hare and

Emily's dodgems piled into the back of him, doof, thunk.

'Stop, in the name of Krull!' said the soldier. Looking at all the skull and crossbones badges on his battle-scarred armour and all the guns and power-swords he was carrying, Emily guessed that he must be one of Lord Krull's Space Commandos. More of them appeared, surrounding the dodgem cars.

'Have you found Colin, Son of Krull?' they demanded.

'Not yet,' said Jinks. 'We're still looking, though . . .'

'Lord Krull grows impatient,' said another soldier. 'He thinks it might help you to concentrate if we blew up a few of your pathetic funfair rides.'

'You mustn't do that!' said Emily.

The first soldier was looking at Jinks's dodgem car as if he had only just noticed it. 'What are these strange vehicles?' he asked.

'These are dodgem cars,' said Emily. 'You drive about in them and bump each other. It's fun.'

'Emily,' said Jinks, 'these are ruthless, highly trained Space Commandos. I don't think they're going to be distracted by dodgem cars.'

But the Space Commandos were looking at each other uncertainly.

'Fun?' they asked.

'Try it!' said Emily, climbing out of her dodgem. Jinks and O'Hare got out of theirs, too, and the soldiers climbed warily into the little cars, gripping the steering wheels. One of them must have found the foot pedal, because his car shot forward and slammed into the bumper of the car in front.

'Ooh, that is kind of fun!' he said.

'Don't think you can distract us from our mission with your pathetic pastimes,' snapped the first soldier, but just then one of the others drove full tilt into his car. 'Ooof! I'll get you for that, Corporal Scarfist!'

'Can't catch me!' the corporal jeered, spinning his dodgem about and zooming off through the crowds with the others close behind him.

As the sounds of bumpers colliding faded, the remaining Space Commandos looked hopefully at Emily.

WAHEY!

'Do we get a go?' they asked. 'Are there any more little cars?'

'There's a whole arena full of them back up the path a way,' she said. 'And there's loads of other things you can do, too. Why not have a go on the teacups?'

She pointed to the nearby ride, where giant teacups went twirling around and around a track. Jinks waved to the lady who was operating them, and she brought the cups to a standstill and invited the Space Commandos aboard. They sat down gingerly on the seats,

as if they were expecting the ride to
be a trap, but once the cups started to
move they soon relaxed. 'Wheeee!' they
shouted, as they went whirling around.

Jinks beckoned to O'Hare and Emily.
'I owe you an apology, Emily,' he said,
as they tiptoed away. 'It turns out
highly trained Space Commandos *can* be
distracted by dodgem cars. Well done!'

Emily beamed. She was so proud that she felt as if she was floating, like one of the silvery balloons the balloon-sellers sold.

They took a short-cut between the swingboats and soon reached the ghost train. It seemed to be working normally again; cars full of passengers were trundling in at one end and out at the other, and nobody was asking for their money back.

'Are the ghosts back at work?' Emily asked Stan.

'No,' said Stan, helping them aboard a pod. 'But apparently there's some spiny, black, rustly things in there. They're not as scary as your actual ghosts, but everyone says they're quite spooky. She's very good, this assistant of yours, Mr Jinks.'

'Assistant?' huffed Jinks, as the pod rolled on its way towards the ghost train entrance. 'Emily isn't our assistant!

Wherever did he get that idea?'

Emily looked the other way and pretended she hadn't heard. Pinned to the wall beside the track where the pod ran were lots of photos of other pods and their passengers. They were pictures taken by automatic cameras of the terrified visitors emerging at the other end of the ride: if you wanted, you could buy a framed one of yourself as a souvenir, or have it printed on a T-shirt under the slogan *I've Been Haunted At Funfair Moon.* Busy ignoring Jinks's question, Emily watched the scared faces go by, until she noticed one which wasn't scared. In fact, it was kind of familiar. A small plump man had been photographed sitting in the back of one of the pods, looking grumpy and unimpressed. He hadn't been

wearing his Funfair Inspector's uniform or his massive Funfair Inspector's hat, and he had been wearing a very unconvincing fake moustache, but she was pretty sure that he was Mr Moonbottom.

She remembered what Stan had said about the grumpy passenger who had ridden the train last week. Could it have been Mr Moonbottom? Maybe it had been his day off. But the Funfair Inspector didn't like funfairs, so why would he visit one in his free time? And why wear a fake moustache? Emily would have thought he'd prefer to stay at home with his Peladorian Puffball pets.

It was all Most Mysterious. As the pod carried them through the curtain of cobwebs into the haunted mansion, Emily decided she would have to have another look at the photo when she came out, and make absolutely sure that it *was* Mr Moonbottom before she mentioned it to Jinks and O'Hare.

NINE

Just inside the mansion, the pod stopped.
Jinks, O'Hare, and Emily jumped out,
and Jinks led the way to another of those
doors marked STAFF ONLY. Behind
it was a staircase, nothing like the dark,
dusty, cobwebby staircases in the rest of
the mansion. This one was quite clean
and well lit, with pictures on the walls.
They climbed it, and knocked on a door
at the top.

'Wh—who's there?' asked a scared-
sounding voice.

'Jinks and O'Hare,' said Jinks.

IS WHERE THE HAUNT IS

'And Emily,' said Emily.

The door opened, and they walked through into the ghosts' living room. There was a TV, some comfy-looking chairs, and pictures on the walls. But mostly there were ghosts: big ones and small ones, some looking like king-sized duvet versions of See-through George, others like walking skeletons or transparent people in old-fashioned clothes. See-through George himself came shooting out of the little crowd to wrap Emily in a ghostly hug.

WOOOOF!

HAPPY HAUNTS

HOW TO CROCHET WITH COBWEBS!

'This is Emily!' he said. 'This is the girl who saved me from the Rustlers!'

'And this is Jinks and O'Hare,' said Emily. 'They've come to get to the bottom of this mystery.'

'We're not scared of Rustlers,' said Jinks, while O'Hare and Emily struck Brave and Resourceful poses.

'Oooh, they're so brave and resourceful!' said the ghosts, looking on admiringly.

'Now,' said Jinks, 'Emily told me that young George here said the Rustlers came up through the floor. Is that right?'

'I saw them!' said a lady ghost, drifting forward. Emily guessed this must be Headless Maude. She wasn't really headless, though; she had a very nice head, it was just that it wasn't attached to her neck; she was carrying it in a sort of handbag with an opening for her face to look out of. 'I saw them coming up through the loose floorboards in the

Haunted Kitchen!'

'Will you show us?' asked Jinks.

The ghosts all looked very worried, but at last See-through George came over and put his ghostly hand in Emily's living one. 'I'll show you,' he said.

'Good lad!' said Jinks. 'That's the spirit, young spirit!'

They made their way back downstairs with See-through George billowing above them like a small flag, if small flags carried cuddly penguins. Some cars full of school children were just going by when they stepped out of the STAFF ONLY door, and O'Hare had fun startling them, throwing his big hairy shadow up the walls and making hideous groans. 'No time for that, O'Hare,' said

Jinks crossly (but Emily could tell that he thought it was funny, too).

The Haunted Kitchen was just as big and shadowy as the rest of the mansion, with a maze of rusty pipes running up the wall and across the ceiling. Drips fell spookily into a basin of cold water, and heaps of dirty washing-up were piled up on the draining board. There was a big, covered dish on the table. 'When the cars come through,' said See-through George, 'Uncle Reg is supposed to lift the cover off, and Headless Maude's head is underneath. You should hear them scream when she sticks her tongue out at them! But when they came down

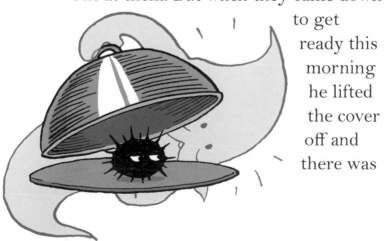 to get ready this morning he lifted the cover off and there was

a Rustler underneath. He screamed even louder!'

O'Hare went over to the corner and lifted a loose floorboard. Underneath was a hatch marked SECRET. Underneath the hatch was a dark shaft, with a metal ladder going down into it.

'It must lead down into the old access tunnels which run under the fair,' said Jinks. 'I'm surprised anyone even knows they're down there. They haven't been used since my grandmother's day.'

'Is that where the Rustlers live, do you think?' asked Emily, looking nervously down the shaft.

'Let's find out,' said Jinks, and started climbing down. The washing-up piles beside the sink were starting to rattle as another car approached, so he said, 'Distract them, See-through George!'

See-through George gave Emily his penguin to hold and floated across the kitchen to hang just in front of the door

as the car full of
children came in.
They were far too
busy screaming to
notice Emily and
O'Hare climbing
down through the
hole in the floor, and
once the car had
gone on its way into
the next room, See-through
George came down the shaft after them.

It was dark at the bottom, and Emily
was a bit scared, but then Jinks and
O'Hare turned their torches on and she
saw that they were standing in a sort
of passage. Just an ordinary, boring
passage, with white walls, and lino on
the floor.

'Hmmm,' said Jinks. He was peering
at a map which was pinned to the wall.
'Let's head that way. It should lead us
underneath the Space Twizzler; that's

where the trouble started this morning.

They started walking, or, in See-through George's case, floating. They passed some other passages branching off, and some other shafts, which must lead up into other rides, but there was no sign of spiny creatures. Then, from one of the side-passages, they caught a faint sound.

A clink of metal on metal. A faint, faint rustling.

'Ooooo-err,' said See-through George.

Emily knew how he felt. But she told herself she wasn't scared as long as Jinks and O'Hare were there, so she took George's hand again and they went after the repairmen down the new passage. The floor of this passage sloped quite steeply downwards, so she guessed that they were descending deep inside Funfair Moon. Pretty soon the walls weren't painted white any more; they were just bare moonrock. Little

stalactites dangled from the ceiling.

Soon, Jinks and O'Hare switched off their torches. It wasn't dark without them. There was light coming from somewhere ahead. They hurried on, and came out into a huge, bright room. It was full of Rustlers. The sound of their rustling filled the big room like the sea.

'What's going on here, then?' asked Jinks, in a voice as loud and stern as a Space Commando's.

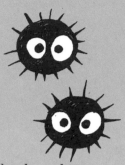

The Rustlers all stopped what they
were doing. An instant later, they had
vanished. There was a tremendous
rustling, a blur of black
movement, and they
had gone.

In the silence,
a cupboard
went, 'Mmmf
mmf mmmf!'

'Why is that cupboard going,
"Mmmf mmf mmmf"?' asked Emily.

O'Hare leaped across the room and

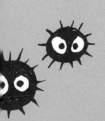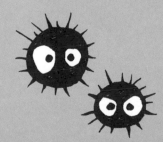

flung the cupboard door open. It was
quite a large cupboard, and looked quite
comfy inside—there were cushions
and things, and a big TV. Sitting on
the cushions and watching the TV was
a small, dark-haired boy. Emily had
thought that he was gagged, and that
was why he had gone, 'Mmmf mmf
mmmf!', but when she got a proper look

at him she realized he had just been trying to say, 'What's going on?' while eating an enormous slice of cake.

'What's going on?' he said again, putting the cake down this time. 'Where have the servants gone?'

'Servants?' asked Emily.

'I thought they must be servants,' said Colin, Son of Krull. 'They brought me here, and gave me cake and things when I asked, like servants do. Are they yours?'

'Those weren't servants!' Emily said. 'Those were kidnappers! You were kidnapped, and you didn't even know it!'

'Oh,' said the boy. He looked disappointed.

'Didn't the creatures explain why they'd taken you?' asked Jinks. 'Didn't they say what they wanted?'

Colin shrugged. 'Why don't you ask them yourselves?'

Emily and her friends turned around.

While they had been talking to Colin, the Rustlers had got over their shock. From their hiding places in the nooks and crannies of the walls they had come silently out, and now a great spiny crowd stood watching, softly rustling to themselves.

'Who are you?' demanded Jinks. 'Why have you come here? Why did you break our rides, and kidnap this child?'

The Rustlers rustled. They spread towards the cupboard like a spiky oil-slick. They weren't very big, but there were an awful lot of them. Emily started to feel a little bit afraid, even though Jinks and O'Hare were with her. She could hear See-through George's see-through teeth chattering. Even Jinks was starting to look nervous.

But O'Hare wasn't having any of that. He took a deep breath, then scared the Rustlers just the way he'd scared those kids back in the Ghost Train.

'Raaaargh!' He jumped forward roaring, stretching his arms out wide, and the Rustlers rolled away with nervous crackling noises and little startled squeaks.

This time, though, they didn't vanish to their hiding places. They clustered in black clumps in the corners of the room, then slowly started to gather together again. They began to climb on top of one another. Their spines interlocked. They made a sound like the sound you'd hear if you quickly undid the velcro tabs on your shoes and recorded the noise, then played it backwards, slowly.

The Rustlers piled themselves up in
wobbling towers, in spiny pyramids
which slumped against one another and
combined to make bigger pyramids.
They formed a spiky figure; a big round
body, balanced on two leg-like Rustler-
towers. It spread out long spiky arms,
which were chains of Rustlers. It looked
like a prickly black shadow of O'Hare.

'RAAAAAARGH!' it roared.

'Hmmm,' said Jinks.

O'Hare raised an eyebrow.

'What shall we do?' asked Emily.

'Run!' said Jinks.

WAIT
FOR
ME!

They ran, Emily in the lead, Colin behind her, Jinks and O'Hare bringing up the rear, while See-through George flapped along above them. They dashed back into the corridor. The Rustlers tried to follow them, but now that they were all stuck together they didn't fit through the doorway any more; the rustling giant collapsed and swirled about in spiny confusion for a moment, then formed itself into a new shape—a Rustler-snake. It came hissing and crinkling behind Emily and her friends as they dashed back towards the surface.

TEN

They didn't bother looking for the ladder
they had come down. With the Rustlers
close behind them, they ran to the first
ladder they saw and scrambled up it as
fast as they could. When Emily popped
open the hatch at the top, she saw that
they were in the middle of the main
fairway, not far from Terror Mountain.
The carousels were tootling, the
waltzers were whirling, and everything
looked pretty much normal. But when
she scrambled out, and pulled Colin out
behind her, there was a sudden shout.

'Krull-va!' Lord Krull came striding through the crowds and gathered Colin up in a big, armoured hug.

'Hello, Dad!' said Colin.

'Are you all right?' the space-lord asked. 'If these fools have harmed you I shall obliterate their puny moon!'

'Oh, don't do that, Dad!' said Colin.

'Certainly not,' snapped another voice. 'Obliterating puny moons is a job for the Galactic Council's planning department, not you, Lord Krull.'

Mr Moonbottom stepped out of the

crowd. He was wearing a white bandage
around his head, but other than that he
looked as if had recovered completely
from the fudge-splosion. He had put his
hat on top of the bandage, which made
the hat look bigger than ever. Miss
Weebly was behind him, as usual. She
started to wave when she saw Emily, but
stopped when Mr Moonbottom gave her
a hard stare.

'And who are you,' roared Lord Krull,
'to tell ME what I can do?'

'Jeremy Moonbottom of the Galactic
Council (Leisure & Entertainment Sub-
Committee),' said Mr Moonbottom,
holding up his badge.

'I shall cut you to pieces!' said Lord
Krull, and reached for his power-sword.

'Oh, I wouldn't do that if I were you,'
said Mr Moonbottom. 'Cutting council
officials to pieces is against regulations.
You'll have to complete a full Risk
Assessment and fill in form R-176 (B). If

you strike me down, the paperwork will be more time-consuming than you can possibly imagine.'

Lord Krull lowered his sword and stood fuming. He hated filling in forms.

Mr Moonbottom turned his attention

to Emily and her friends. Jinks and O'Hare had climbed out of the hatch now, and they were sitting on its lid. Every now and then the lid gave a sort of jolt, as if someone or something was shoving it from below.

'Don't tell me something else has gone wrong?' he said gloatingly, as if that was exactly what he wanted them to tell him.

'No,' said Jinks, struggling to hold the lid shut.

'Everything's fine,' said Emily.

Mr Moonbottom sniffed. 'I don't believe you. Not only is this the most badly-run funfair I've ever inspected, but I believe it's infested with black, spiky creatures!'

'We haven't seen any black, spiky creatures, have we Mr Jinks?' squeaked Emily.

'No, not at all,' said Jinks, and then added, 'Ooops!' The lid beneath him burst open, he and O'Hare went flying

into the air, and a geyser of Rustlers came shooting out of the open hatch.

Everyone jumped backwards in alarm as the Rustlers bounced across the grass, rebounded off the roundabouts, and quickly started gathering themselves into a great, dark mass again.

'I knew it!' crowed Mr Moonbottom. He had dropped his briefcase again and he was scrabbling around on the grass, gathering up his fallen sandwiches and papers. He paused to point at the bouncing Rustlers. 'There they are! Black, spiky things, as large as life and twice as pointy! That's the last straw! I declare Funfair Moon CLOSED!'

'No!' wailed Emily.

'That's not fair!' shouted Colin.

Jinks and O'Hare didn't say anything. They were watching as the Rustlers formed themselves into another prickly giant. Towering above the roundabouts, the monster waved its arms and roared as if it was getting ready to flatten the two repairmen, and then the rest of the fair.

'There won't be much of Funfair Moon left to close, once that thing starts rampaging,' muttered Jinks. 'Stand back, everybody!'

O'Hare tried doing his 'Rargh!' thing again, but the spiky giant wasn't frightened of him any more. Why should it be, thought Emily. It was twenty times taller than O'Hare. Nothing would frighten it now . . . unless . . .

She turned and ran as fast as she could to where a dodgem car stood (it must have been abandoned there by one of the Space Commandos). Then she drove as fast as she could back

to Terror Mountain. The candyfloss monster still lay where they had left it, but it was starting to twitch in its sleep and grumble. The roller coaster staff were watching it uneasily, and arguing over which of them should be the one to shoot it with more tranquillizer darts.

Emily pushed past them. She ran up to the candyfloss creature and poked it. 'Hey!' she shouted. 'Do you want a fight?'

The monster raised its pink flossy head and blinked at her. It tried out a sleepy growl, which turned into a roar. A gale of candyfloss-scented breath nearly blew Emily off her feet.

'Not me!' she shouted, as the creature started scrambling to its feet and swiped at her with one huge pink hand. 'Pick on someone your own size!'

And she pointed across the roofs of the rides to where the spiky black giant towered.

The candyfloss creature glowered at it.
It scratched its head and got its finger
stuck and had to tug it free.

'You may be just a lot of angry pink
candyfloss,' said Emily, 'but Funfair

Moon is your home, and those creatures
are going to get it closed down! What
are you going to do about that, eh?'

The ground shuddered as the
candyfloss monster stepped over her
and started shoving its way between the
rides. Emily jumped back in her dodgem
car and drove after it as fast as she
could, trying not to get the car stuck in
its big, sticky footprints.

'Come on, Candyfloss!' she yelled.
People who had been hurrying away
from the Rustlers stopped and turned
back to watch as the candyfloss monster
lumbered out onto the fairway. The
Rustlers lurched towards it.

MWARRR!

They swung one rustly
fist in a huge punch, right
in the monster's belly,
but the fist sunk into the
candyfloss and stuck there.

The Rustlers reached out
one rustling foot, trying
to trip up the candyfloss
creature.

The foot stuck fast too.

The candyfloss
monster raised
a huge fist, and
slammed it down
on the Rustlers.
They scattered in
every direction,
no longer a
giant, just a cascade
of scared Rustlers.

'Thank you!' shouted Emily.

'That's all right,' mumbled the
candyfloss monster shyly.

'Don't think this means I'll be
changing my mind,' snapped Mr
Moonbottom. 'Those spiky creatures are
a pest. You may have scattered them, but
they'll keep on making rides go wrong!'

'Er, no, actually,' said a small voice
behind him. Miss Weebly had her hand
up. 'Actually they won't. Not if we tell
them nicely to stop.'

'You keep out of this, Weebly!' snapped

the Funfair Inspector.

'But I know what those creatures are,' said Miss Weebly. 'I was reading all about them in that very interesting book of yours, while I was waiting at the Lost Property Office for you to wake up.'

'Book?' spluttered Mr Moonbottom. 'What book?'

'*How to Keep and Care for Your Peladorian Puffball*. Here it is!' She reached down and picked up the book, which was still lying in the grass near the Inspector's feet. She held it up so that everyone could see it. From the front cover a cute and cuddly Puffball smiled back at them.

'But these Rustlers don't look anything like that!' said Emily. One of the spiky creatures was hiding nearby in the shadows under the Flying Pony Carousel. She could see it shivering there, the sharp pinpoints of its spines a-glitter. She had never seen anything that looked less like a lovely, fluffy Peladorian Puffball.

'The spiky form is just the first phase of their development,' said Miss Weebly. 'In the valleys of the planet Pelador, where they hatch, there are all sorts of fierce creatures waiting to eat them, so they have developed this coat of spines. When they are old enough, they learn how to band together, and that allows them to climb to the high mountain pastures, where they change into a new form. They make perfect pets because they'll do anything their owner tells them to.'

Emily watched the Rustler beneath the carousel. It was quivering more and more quickly. Suddenly, with a sort of soft popping sound, it changed. The hard black stuff which had covered its spines flew off in a cloud of tiny splinters, and soft fur exploded from beneath.

'Meep!' said the Rustler, rolling out into the light. It looked like a delighted pom-pom now.

'Meep! Meep! Meep!' other Puffballs were going, in the shadows and the narrow spaces between the rides, and people in the crowd were saying, 'Aaaahhh!' as they caught sight of the new creatures and saw how cute they looked.

'But how did they get all the way from Pelador to Funfair Moon?' asked Jinks, taking his hat off and scratching his head.

Emily pointed at Mr Moonbottom. 'I think he brought them here,' she said.

'Gasp!' went everyone except Emily and Mr Moonbottom. Mr Moonbottom went, 'Who, me?'

'Yes!' said Emily. 'You came here last week, in disguise. There's a picture of you riding the ghost train. I bet you went on the Space Twizzler and the Merry-Go-Round and loads of other rides too, and wherever you went you left some baby Puffballs!'

Mr Moonbottom turned an interesting shade of purplish red. 'And why would I do that, little girl?'

Emily said, 'Because you enjoy shutting funfairs down! But you knew Jinks and O'Hare keep Funfair Moon running so well that you'd never find a reason, so you decided to make a reason! You planted those poor Puffballs here and told them to make trouble so that there'd be lots going wrong when you came to inspect us!'

'That's absolutely . . . I mean to say . . . How dare you suggest that . . .' spluttered the Funfair Inspector. Then he said, 'All right! It's TRUE!'

Everyone said, 'Gasp!' again. Even Emily. Even the candyfloss monster. Even the Puffballs, peeking from their hiding places.

'I HATE FUNFAIRS!' bellowed Mr Moonbottom. 'What a waste of time they are! People sliding down helter-skelters and twirling round and round on roundabouts. What's the point of that? Entertainment? Pah! Entertainment should educate people, and prepare them for the real world!

And that's why I set up my own theme park. It's called OFFICE WORLD. It's a place where visitors can enjoy rides that introduce them to the joy of filing and the thrills of double-entry book-keeping. A sensible theme park for today's galaxy!'

OFFICE WORLD!

SENSIBLE FUN FOR THE WHOLE FAMILY!

RIDE THE SWIVEL CHAIR ROLLER COASTER!

THE TOWER OF FILING!

THE PAPERCLIP PARADE

TEA-TROLLEY LAGOON

'Office World?' said Lord Krull. 'I've never heard of it.'

'Nobody has,' said Mr Moonbottom bitterly. 'Nobody ever came to visit it.'

'I'm not surprised,' whispered Miss Weebly to Emily.

'No,' the Funfair Inspector went on. 'They were all too busy frittering their time away at Funfair Moon. So I decided the only thing to do was close you down for good, and that's what I've done. Don't think you've beaten me. I've already gathered all the evidence I need to close this place for good. It's all stored in my computer-hat.'

Emily looked at his huge hat again. What she had thought were little decorative studs were really camera lenses and microphones. He must have been recording everything, she realized—or, at least, all the bits which made Funfair Moon look bad.

Mr Moonbottom laughed. 'All I need

to do is get back to my spaceship and transmit this information to the Galactic Council,' he said. 'Then you'll be officially shut down!'

'But I'll tell them it's all a lie!' said Miss Weebly.

'Oh, will you, Wendy?' sneered the Funfair Inspector. 'You can try, I suppose—but that will mean filling in Form Z-B-4876/L. In triplicate!'

Miss Weebly gasped. 'Not Form Z-B-4876/L! That could take years!'

'Exactly,' sneered Mr Moonbottom. 'By the time this place is allowed to reopen, everyone will have forgotten about it. They'll all be having the time of their lives at Office World, and I'll be rich! So long, you twits!'

And he leaped into Emily's dodgem car and went shooting off through the crowd.

'Quick!' shouted Jinks. 'After him!'

'Where is he going?' asked See-through George.

'His spaceship!' said Emily. 'It's parked near the main entrance!'

'We'll never get there in time!' said Jinks.

O'Hare just turned round and looked at the candyfloss creature, but it seemed to have gone to sleep again. Then he looked at Lord Krull's Space Commandos, and shrugged.

O'Hare could put a lot of meaning into a shrug. This one was the sort of shrug that meant, *Can we borrow your jetpacks?*

ELEVEN

Only three of the commandos had jetpacks. Jinks took one, O'Hare took another, and Emily helped herself to the third before they could tell her not to. Everyone else followed on foot, hurrying towards the entrance.

It turned out that jetpacks were quite hard to steer. Jinks and O'Hare must have done it before, because they took off in a straight line, but Emily went spiralling across the fair and zoomed past a surprised podful of visitors in the giant Ferris wheel. 'That looks fun!'

they shouted. 'Where can we get one
of those?' But before she could explain,
the jetpack went into a dive and took
her swooping down towards the waters
of the Mermaid Lagoon. Just before she
hit the water a friendly voice beside her
said, 'Pull back on the red lever!'

She looked round. See-through George
was flying beside her, still clutching
his penguin. She found the red
lever on the controls and pulled it
back. The toes of her sneakers
cut v-shaped wakes across the
surface of the lagoon as the
jetpack flew upwards again,
and the mermaids cheered
and waved.

'How did you know about the red lever?' she asked, when they were safely above the level of the roundabouts and swing-boats.

George waved a pamphlet at her.

It was the jetpack instruction manual.

'Now use the blue lever to steer!' he said.

Soon they were flying side by side. 'Look!' said Emily, as they shot through the archways of Sheikh Rattle's Rock-'n'-Roll-O-Coaster. Down below them, Mr Moonbottom's dodgem car went bouncing through the alleyways between the snack bars and amusement arcades. He was halfway to his boring spaceship. Emily couldn't see Jinks and O'Hare anywhere, and she was a bit uncertain about tackling the Funfair Inspector on her own.

Then she looked at all the flickering lights and whirling roundabouts spread out beneath her. A couple of Space Commandos were wandering away from the shooting gallery, weighed down by all the cuddly toys they'd won. A hollowed-out log full of screeching cub scouts came whooshing down the log-flume and splashed into the water, throwing up a wave that filled with rainbows in the light from the big sign outside the Hall of Mirrors. This place is FUN, Emily thought to herself. It's silly and noisy and it isn't educational, but it's pretty and it's fun and I love it, and I will NEVER let Mr Moonbottom close it!

She checked the instruction manual which See-through George was holding in front of her, and put the jetpack into a dive, straight at Mr Moonbottom.

Mr Moonbottom was just zooming past the Space Twizzler when he heard the swoosh of the jetpack. He looked up in time to see Emily come swooping out of the sky. 'Aaaargh!' they both said. Then she hit him. The empty dodgem car went pootling on and crashed into a fortune teller's tent. ('I knew that was going to happen!' shouted the fortune teller, from under the collapsing canvas.)

Emily and Mr Moonbottom landed on the grass outside the entrance to the Space Twizzler. Emily's jetpack came off. So did Mr Moonbottom's hat. It rolled across the ground, and Emily scrambled after it.

'Give that back!' shouted the Funfair Inspector.

'No!' shouted Emily, sitting on it.

See-through George came down and hovered beside her. 'It's three against one,' he said. 'You should give up, Mr Moonbottom.'

'Give up?' scoffed Mr Moonbottom. 'Because of a girl, and a ghostie? And what do you mean, "three against one"? There's only two of you!'

See-through George waved Penguin at him.

The Funfair Inspector wasn't impressed. 'Give that hat here!' he growled.

'No you don't, Moonbottom,' said Jinks, coming down out of the sky nearby.

Mr Moonbottom hesitated, then started to advance on Emily again. Emily looked up. In the sky above the Funfair Inspector, O'Hare was hovering like a big, furry balloon. Emily waved at him. He grinned at her, and shrugged. Then he turned off his jetpack.

SPUDGE. He landed on top of Mr Moonbottom, and covered him completely. For a moment she was afraid O'Hare had squashed him flat,

but muffled, furious shouts emerged, so she knew he was all right.

'Sorry about our late arrival,' said Jinks, taking off his hat and brushing some dust off it. 'We took a wrong turning. Good work, Emily!'

Emily beamed, and hugged See-through George. It was like cuddling a cloud.

Other people were starting to arrive. Colin and his dad, Amy Peeploid and her parents, a crowd of curious fairgoers and Space Commandos. Peladorian Puffballs bounded and bounced around their feet like over-excited furry footballs. Even

the other ghosts had come out of the
Ghost Train to see what was going on.

Miss Weebly came pushing her way to
the front, and the Commandos got their
guns ready as O'Hare carefully stood up,
revealing the cross and crumpled form
of Mr Moonbottom.

'You're under arrest, sir!' she said. 'I'm
going to take you back to
Galactic Council HQ.'

Mr Moonbottom
got up. He looked
at his hat, which
Jinks was very
carefully taking
to pieces. He
looked at Lord Krull,

MEEP!

who stood with his arms folded, as if daring Mr Moonbottom to try and run away.

'Oh, very well,' he said.

'I hope you're very sorry,' said Miss Weebly, as sternly as she could. 'It's our job to make sure that funfairs are safe and fun, not close them down and set up boring office-themed replacements.'

'I am sorry,' said Mr Moonbottom, hanging his head. And everyone had been having so much fun that they were ready to forgive him; they cheered and laughed, and shouted, 'That's all right— don't do it again!' But Mr Moonbottom wasn't really sorry. He was one

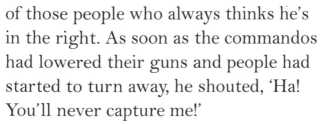

of those people who always thinks he's in the right. As soon as the commandos had lowered their guns and people had started to turn away, he shouted, 'Ha! You'll never capture me!'

Before anyone could stop him, he ran through the entrance to the helter-skelter. Lord Krull started to go after him, but O'Hare held him back. Jinks said, 'Careful!'

'Ha ha!' shouted Moonbottom, running towards the foot of the slide. 'The candyfloss will break my fall, and I'll be out of this place long before you muppets can catch up with me!'

He dived onto the slide and shot up it. Emily looked up, and saw his tiny shape go shooting off the top of the helter-skelter with a wild, 'Wa-hoooo!'

'What did he mean, the candyfloss will break his fall?' asked a large green alien standing next to Emily. It was Figgis, the owner of the Space Twizzler.

'Mr Moonbottom may be a villain, but he didn't want anyone getting seriously hurt,' said Jinks. 'When he got his Puffball friends to reverse your helter-skelter, they must have turned it round a bit to make sure that anyone who flies off the top of it will get a soft landing. It's aimed straight at the candyfloss vats.'

Figgis shook his head. 'Not any more it's not,' he said.

'What do you mean?'

'I noticed someone had turned it round. I just turned it back.'

'So what is it pointing at now?' asked Emily.

Across the fairground came drifting a long scream and a loud, soft

DOOF.

It was the sound of a funfair inspector
falling from a great height into one of
Funfair Moon's enormous rubbish bins.

TWELVE

Mr Moonbottom was lucky; the pile of rubbish broke his fall, and Jinks and O'Hare fished him out of the bin before it was taken away for recycling. Once he'd been hosed down he didn't even smell too bad.

'What will you tell the Galactic Council (Leisure and Entertainment Sub-Committee) about us, Miss Weebly?' Emily asked, as they watched Lord Krull's Space Commandos handcuff him and march him aboard the Official Spaceship. 'I'm afraid a lot has gone wrong today—it isn't always like this.'

'I'm sure it isn't,' said Miss Weebly.

'And we do have an infestation of Peladorian Puffballs . . .'

'Yes, but I don't think anyone will mind now that they've grown out of their spiky phase, and you've told them to stop doing all the bad things Mr Moonbottom ordered them to,' smiled Miss Weebly.

The Puffballs had all grown very fond of O'Hare, perhaps because he was even rounder and hairier than them. They followed him about in a happy crowd, but they never seemed to mind when somebody else picked them up and gave them a cuddle. Emily guessed they hadn't had many cuddles before, what with being all spiky and everything. Maybe they were making up for lost time.

'But what are we going to do with
them all, O'Hare?' asked Jinks. 'They
can't come and live in our little house,
there isn't room.'

O'Hare just shrugged, and passed him
a Puffball to cuddle.

The candyfloss creature was awake
again. It was much calmer now, and
it was helping the owners of Terror
Mountain to repair some of the damage

it had done. Emily thought it looked quite cool, scrambling about on the crags of the giant roller coaster. Maybe they could ask it to stay, and pretend to menace all the roller coaster rides.

Colin was looking at Terror Mountain too. He tugged at Lord Krull's gauntlet. 'Dad, Dad, can we go on the roller coaster?'

'Hmmm,' said Lord Krull, nervously.
'I am not sure . . . It's nearly your
bedtime . . .'

'Oh, come on!' said Emily. 'We should all
go on it! It will be fun!'

So they did.

And it was.

And after that they went on the trampolines, and the aeroplanes, and the swing-boats, and went rowing on

the mermaid lagoon, and Emily thought
how pretty Funfair Moon looked, all
lit up under the midnight sky, and how
amazing it was that you could make
something so magical out of just wood
and metal and machinery and coloured
lights.

But the most amazing bit came right at the end, when Mr Jinks said, 'Come on young Emily, time for bed.'

Emily tried to say she wasn't tired, but she was yawning so much she couldn't get the words out, so she said goodnight to See-through George and arranged to meet him again tomorrow, and said goodbye to Colin and promised to take him on the ghost train the next time his

dad brought him to Funfair Moon. Then she let Jinks and O'Hare lead her to where their little car was waiting.

They flew her home to the Lost Property Office. Mrs Mimms was already asleep, so they didn't bother waking her, they just set the car to hover outside while they all climbed in through Emily's bedroom window. Emily went into the bathroom to brush her teeth and change into her pyjamas. When she came back, Jinks and O'Hare were still there. O'Hare was looking at Emily's model funfair; Jinks was just looking awkward.

O'Hare gave Jinks a shrug which meant, *Go on then—tell her!*

'Er, well,' said Jinks. 'I just wanted to say that we couldn't have managed without you today, young Emily. You've got the makings of a very good funfair repairer. Any time you're not at school, and you feel like helping us, we'd be glad

to have you on our team. That is, if you
want to be . . .'

'Of course I do!' shouted Emily.

O'Hare gave her a huge, hairy hug.
Then he pulled something out of his
toolbox.

'What's that, O'Hare?' said Jinks. 'Oh, it's the manual for the skelter-helter. I mean, helter-skelter. Our first job tomorrow is to get it working properly again.'

O'Hare held the manual out to Jinks.

'What?' said Jinks.

O'Hare gave him a look.

'Ah, well, I guess now is as good a time to start as any,' said Jinks. He sat down on the end of Emily's bed, opened the book, and began to read.

'How to fix your helter-skelter in five easy steps. First, let's check some standard guidelines. No matter what type and make of helter-skelter, basic principles remain the same . . .'

CLOTILDA MAXIMUS HELTER SKELTER MODEL NO. DX-4062

Emily got into bed. There was a Peladorian Puffball already in there, sleeping soundly, like a fluffy hot water bottle. (Those Puffballs had got everywhere!) She snuggled up to it and listened to Jinks read, while the lights of the funfair flickered through the open window, and the noise of the funfair lulled her off to sleep.

When she woke, it was morning.
Emily smiled, remembering yesterday's
adventures, and all the brilliant stuff
that had happened. Then she sat up with
a start—what if it had all been a dream?

She jumped out of bed and ran to the
window. She opened the curtains. There
on the sill sat her Peladorian Puffball,
basking in the morning sun. Outside,
Jinks and O'Hare were already hard at
work. They had propped a ladder up
against the front of their house and Jinks
was shouting directions from below
while O'Hare teetered on the top with a
paintbrush.

There was a new sign above their door.

★ PHILIP ★ REEVE

CAN INVENT ALIEN WORLDS FASTER THAN YOU CAN SAY :FUDGESPLOSION: ON THE RARE OCCASIONS WHEN GRAVITY INVERTS ON PLANET EARTH YOU CAN FIND HIM FLOATING OVER DARTMOOR, LOOKING THOUGHTFUL

SARAH McINTYRE

IS NEVER HAPPIER THAN WHEN SHE'S HANGING UPSIDE DOWN OR PLUMMETING THROUGH SPACE. SHE LOVES THINKING UP STORY IDEAS WITH REEVE, AND HE WAFTED HIS WAY OVER TO HER STUDIO IN LONDON TO HELP HER WITH SOME OF THE ARTWORK IN THE EARLY STAGES OF THE BOOK.

CAKES IN SPACE
BY PHILIP REEVE AND SARAH McINTYRE

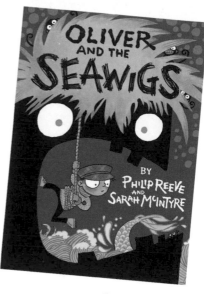

OLIVER AND THE SEAWIGS
BY PHILIP REEVE AND SARAH McINTYRE

PUGS OF THE FROZEN NORTH
BY PHILIP REEVE AND SARAH McINTYRE

CHECK OUT THESE OTHER AWESOME REEVE & McINTYRE ADVENTURES!

A REEVE & McINTYRE PRODUCTION